THE COMPLETE VEGETARIAN ANTI INFLAMMATORY DIET COOKBOOK

Plant Based Recipes To Relieve Rheumatoid Arthritis Pains And Other Inflammations In The Body With Quick Boost To The Immune System

ROSELINE BERKINS

TABLE OF CONTENTS

- Saturated and Trans Fats

- Excessive Dairy

SECTION 1: BREAKFAST

1. Turmeric Spiced Oatmeal

2. Avocado Toast with Cherry Tomatoes

3. Chia Seed Pudding with Mixed Berries

4. Sweet Potato and Spinach Breakfast Burrito

5. Quinoa Breakfast Bowl with Almond Milk

SECTION 2: SOUPS AND STEWS

6. Lentil and Vegetable Soup

7. Ginger Carrot Soup

8. Tomato and Basil Gazpacho

9. Spicy Pumpkin Stew

10. Spinach and White Bean Soup

SECTION 3: SALADS

11. Kale and Quinoa Salad with Lemon-Tahini Dressing

12. Broccoli and Walnut Salad

13. Mediterranean Chickpea Salad

14. Beet and Arugula Salad with Balsamic Vinaigrette

15. Cucumber Avocado Salad with Lime Dressing

SECTION 4: MAIN DISHES

16. Roasted Vegetable Stir-Fry with Tofu

17. Cauliflower and Chickpea Curry

18. Zucchini Noodles with Pesto

19. Sweet Potato and Black Bean Enchiladas

20. Eggplant and Mushroom Lasagna

SECTION 5: SIDES

21. Garlic Roasted Brussels Sprouts

22. Turmeric Roasted Cauliflower

23. Quinoa and Vegetable Stuffed Peppers

24. Lemon Herb Roasted Potatoes

25. Sauteed Green Beans with Almonds

SECTION 6: SNACKS

26. Hummus and Veggie Sticks

27. Spiced Nuts Mix

28. Roasted Chickpeas with Herbs

29. Guacamole with Whole Grain Crackers

30. Greek Yogurt and Berry Parfait

SECTION 7: BEVERAGES

31. Turmeric Golden Milk Latte

32. Green Tea and Ginger Cooler

33. Cucumber Mint Infused Water

34. Berry Smoothie with Flaxseeds

35. Anti-Inflammatory Green Juice

SECTION 8: DESSERTS

36. Turmeric Coconut Bliss Balls

37. Dark Chocolate Avocado Mousse

38. Blueberry Chia Seed Pudding

39. Mango Sorbet with Mint

40. Almond Flour Banana Bread

SECTION 9: BOWLS

SECTION 12: PIZZA

56. Cauliflower Crust Pizza with Roasted Vegetables

57. Mediterranean Pizza with Olives and Feta

58. Spinach and Artichoke Pizza

59. Margherita Pizza with Whole Wheat Crust

60. Sweet Potato and Kale Pizza

INTRODUCTION

What is an Anti-Inflammatory Diet?

An anti-inflammatory diet is a nutritional approach aimed at reducing inflammation in the body, a natural immune response that plays a crucial role in the healing process. While acute inflammation is a normal and protective mechanism, chronic inflammation can lead to various health issues, including cardiovascular diseases, arthritis, and autoimmune disorders.

The anti-inflammatory diet focuses on incorporating foods that have been scientifically proven to minimize inflammation, promoting overall health and well-being. These foods typically include a variety of fruits, vegetables, whole grains, nuts, seeds, and healthy fats. Conversely, the diet discourages the consumption of pro-inflammatory foods such as processed sugars, saturated fats, and refined carbohydrates.

Benefits of Adopting a Vegetarian Approach

Choosing a vegetarian approach to an anti-inflammatory diet offers a multitude of benefits. A vegetarian diet primarily emphasizes plant-based foods, which are rich in antioxidants, phytonutrients, and essential vitamins and minerals. These nutrients play a vital role in neutralizing free radicals and reducing oxidative stress, both of which are linked to chronic inflammation.

Moreover, adopting a vegetarian lifestyle has been associated with lower risks of heart disease, certain cancers, and type 2 diabetes. Vegetarian diets are naturally lower in saturated fats and cholesterol, promoting cardiovascular health. The inclusion of plant-based proteins further contributes to weight management, as they tend to be lower in calories and saturated fats compared to animal-based proteins.

Basics of Inflammation

Inflammation is a complex biological response to harmful stimuli, such as pathogens, damaged cells, or irritants. It is a protective mechanism involving the immune system that aims to eliminate the cause of cell injury, clear out damaged cells and tissues, and initiate tissue repair. The key components of inflammation include increased blood flow, immune cell migration, and the release of signaling molecules.

Acute inflammation is a short-term and localized response that helps the body deal with injuries or infections. Symptoms like redness, heat, swelling, and pain are common indicators of acute inflammation. This process is essential for the body's defense and repair mechanisms.

Chronic Inflammation and its Impact

On the other hand, chronic inflammation is a prolonged and systemic inflammatory response that can have detrimental effects on the body. It is often associated with lifestyle factors such as poor diet, lack of exercise, stress, and environmental factors. Chronic inflammation is linked to various health conditions, including cardiovascular diseases, rheumatoid arthritis, inflammatory bowel diseases, and certain cancers.

Long-term exposure to inflammation can lead to tissue damage and dysfunction, contributing to the development of chronic diseases. Therefore, understanding and managing inflammation through lifestyle choices, including dietary decisions, becomes crucial for overall health and disease prevention.

The introduction to an anti-inflammatory diet underscores the importance of dietary choices in modulating inflammation. By adopting a vegetarian approach and understanding the fundamentals of inflammation, individuals can harness the benefits of a lifestyle that supports long-term health and well-being.

Key Principles of a Vegetarian Anti-Inflammatory Diet

Adopting a Vegetarian Anti-Inflammatory Diet involves three essential principles that not only promote overall health but also specifically target inflammation within the body. These principles focus on choosing whole foods, emphasizing plant-based proteins, and incorporating anti-inflammatory spices and herbs.

Choosing Whole Foods

Whole foods are minimally processed and in their natural state, rich in nutrients that support the body's overall well-being. In a Vegetarian Anti-Inflammatory Diet, the emphasis on whole foods involves incorporating a variety of fruits, vegetables, whole grains, nuts, and seeds. These nutrient-dense options provide essential vitamins, minerals, fiber, and antioxidants, which collectively contribute to reducing inflammation.

Guidelines for Choosing Whole Foods:

- Prioritize fresh fruits and vegetables in a rainbow of colors to ensure a diverse range of nutrients.

- Opt for whole grains like quinoa, brown rice, and oats over refined grains.

- Include a variety of nuts and seeds for healthy fats, protein, and anti-inflammatory properties.

Emphasizing Plant-Based Proteins

Plant-based proteins play a crucial role in a Vegetarian Anti-Inflammatory Diet by providing essential amino acids without the inflammatory effects often associated with certain animal proteins. Legumes, beans, lentils, tofu, tempeh, and edamame are excellent sources of plant-based proteins. These foods not only contribute to inflammation reduction but also support muscle health, satiety, and overall vitality.

Tips for Emphasizing Plant-Based Proteins:

- Include a variety of legumes in your meals, such as chickpeas, black beans, and lentils.

- Experiment with tofu and tempeh as versatile and protein-rich meat substitutes.

- Combine different plant-based protein sources to ensure a well-rounded amino acid profile.

Incorporating Anti-Inflammatory Spices and Herbs

Certain spices and herbs possess powerful anti-inflammatory properties, adding both flavor and health benefits to meals. Incorporating these elements into a Vegetarian Anti-Inflammatory Diet can enhance the overall anti-inflammatory effect. Turmeric, ginger, cinnamon, garlic, and basil are notable examples of ingredients that contain bioactive compounds with anti-inflammatory and antioxidant properties.

Ways to Incorporate Anti-Inflammatory Spices and Herbs:

- Make golden milk by adding turmeric and ginger to warm plant-based milk.

- Use fresh or powdered garlic and ginger in stir-fries, soups, and sauces for added flavor and anti-inflammatory benefits.

- Experiment with cinnamon and basil in both sweet and savory dishes to enhance taste while promoting health.

By consciously choosing whole foods, emphasizing plant-based proteins, and incorporating anti-inflammatory spices and herbs, individuals can create a well-rounded Vegetarian Anti-Inflammatory Diet. This approach not only addresses inflammation but also fosters a lifestyle that prioritizes nutrition, flavor, and long-term well-being.

Foods to Include

1. Fruits and Vegetables

Overview:

Fruits and vegetables are the cornerstone of a vegetarian anti-inflammatory diet, providing a rich array of vitamins, minerals, fiber, and antioxidants. These nutrient-packed foods play a crucial role in reducing inflammation and supporting overall health.

Benefits:

- Antioxidant Power: Fruits and vegetables are rich in antioxidants, such as vitamin C, beta-carotene, and flavonoids, which help neutralize free radicals and reduce oxidative stress.

- Anti-Inflammatory Compounds: Many fruits and vegetables contain anti-inflammatory compounds, such as quercetin in apples and sulforaphane in broccoli.

- Fiber Content: High fiber content promotes gut health, regulates blood sugar levels, and contributes to overall satiety.

Inclusion Tips:

- Aim for a colorful variety to maximize nutrient diversity.

- Prioritize leafy greens, berries, citrus fruits, and cruciferous vegetables.

- Incorporate raw and cooked options for a balance of nutrients.

2. Whole Grains

Overview:

Whole grains are a vital component of a vegetarian anti-inflammatory diet, providing complex carbohydrates, fiber, and essential nutrients. They contribute to sustained energy levels and offer a range of health benefits.

Benefits:

- Fiber-Rich: Whole grains, such as brown rice, quinoa, and oats, are high in fiber, promoting digestive health and supporting weight management.

- Nutrient Density: Whole grains contain B-vitamins, minerals (iron, magnesium), and phytonutrients that contribute to overall well-being.

- Stable Blood Sugar: The complex carbohydrates in whole grains help regulate blood sugar levels, reducing the risk of inflammation.

Inclusion Tips:

- Choose whole grains like brown rice, quinoa, oats, barley, and whole wheat.

- Experiment with ancient grains such as farro, freekeh, and bulgur for variety.

- Limit refined grains like white bread and opt for whole grain alternatives.

3. Legumes and Beans

Overview:

Legumes and beans are excellent plant-based sources of protein, fiber, and various essential nutrients. They play a central role in a vegetarian anti-inflammatory diet, contributing to heart health and inflammation reduction.

Benefits:

- Plant-Based Protein: Legumes provide a protein source without the saturated fat found in animal products, promoting muscle health.

- Fiber Content: High fiber content aids digestion and helps maintain a healthy gut microbiome.

- Nutrient Profile: Legumes offer a range of nutrients, including iron, zinc, and folate.

Inclusion Tips:

- Include a variety of legumes such as lentils, chickpeas, black beans, and edamame.

- Opt for whole, unprocessed legumes when possible, but canned options are convenient too (rinse to reduce sodium).

- Incorporate legumes into salads, soups, stews, and grain bowls.

4. Nuts and Seeds

Overview:

Nuts and seeds are nutrient-dense powerhouses, providing healthy fats, protein, vitamins, and minerals. Including a variety of nuts and seeds in a vegetarian anti-inflammatory diet supports heart health and inflammation reduction.

Benefits:

- Heart-Healthy Fats: Nuts and seeds contain monounsaturated and polyunsaturated fats that promote heart health.

- Omega-3 Fatty Acids: Walnuts, chia seeds, and flaxseeds are rich sources of omega-3 fatty acids, known for their anti-inflammatory properties.

- Protein and Nutrient Boost: Nuts and seeds provide essential nutrients, including magnesium, zinc, and vitamin E.

Inclusion Tips:

- Consume a mix of nuts such as almonds, walnuts, and pistachios.

- Incorporate seeds like chia, flax, pumpkin, and sunflower seeds into smoothies, yogurt, or salads.

- Be mindful of portion sizes due to their calorie density.

5. Healthy Fats

Overview:

Healthy fats are an essential part of a vegetarian anti-inflammatory diet, promoting cardiovascular health and overall well-being. Including sources of monounsaturated and polyunsaturated fats can help balance inflammatory responses in the body.

Benefits:

- Anti-Inflammatory Properties: Healthy fats, particularly omega-3 fatty acids found in fatty fish, flaxseeds, and walnuts, help reduce inflammation.

- Heart Health: Monounsaturated fats, such as those in avocados and olive oil, support cardiovascular health by improving cholesterol levels.

- Brain Function: Omega-3 fatty acids contribute to cognitive function and may reduce the risk of neurodegenerative diseases.

Inclusion Tips:

- Use olive oil as a primary cooking oil and drizzle it on salads.

- Include avocados in salads, wraps, or as a standalone snack.

- Incorporate fatty fish like salmon or trout into your diet or consider plant-based sources of omega-3s.

Remember, a well-rounded vegetarian anti-inflammatory diet focuses on variety and moderation. Experiment with different foods within these categories to create delicious, satisfying, and health-promoting meals. Always consult with a healthcare professional or a registered dietitian for personalized advice based on your specific health needs.

foods to limit or avoid

1. Processed Foods

Processed foods are those that have undergone significant alterations from their original state. They often contain additives, preservatives, and high levels of salt and sugar. While convenient, these foods can contribute to inflammation and negatively impact overall health.

Why Limit Processed Foods:

- High in Additives: Processed foods often contain artificial colors, flavors, and preservatives, which may trigger inflammatory responses in some individuals.

- Added Sugars: Many processed foods are laden with refined sugars, contributing to increased inflammation and potential insulin resistance.

- Increased Sodium Content: Excessive salt in processed foods can lead to water retention and may contribute to inflammation, particularly in those sensitive to sodium.

Alternatives:

- Opt for whole, minimally processed foods.

- Prepare meals at home using fresh ingredients.

- Choose snacks like fruits, vegetables, and nuts instead of packaged snacks.

2. Refined Sugar

Refined sugar, found in sweets, desserts, and many processed foods, has been linked to various health issues, including inflammation. High sugar intake can lead to spikes in blood sugar levels and contribute to chronic inflammation over time.

Why Limit Refined Sugar:

- Blood Sugar Spikes: Refined sugar causes rapid increases in blood sugar levels, triggering an inflammatory response.

- Increased Risk of Chronic Diseases: High sugar consumption is associated with conditions such as obesity, diabetes, and heart disease, all linked to chronic inflammation.

Alternatives:

- Choose natural sweeteners like honey, maple syrup, or agave in moderation.

- Satisfy sweet cravings with whole fruits.

- Read food labels to identify and avoid hidden sources of added sugars.

3. Saturated and Trans Fats

Saturated and trans fats, commonly found in certain oils, fried foods, and processed snacks, can contribute to inflammation and negatively impact heart health.

Why Limit Saturated and Trans Fats:

- Heart Health: Saturated and trans fats raise levels of LDL (bad) cholesterol, contributing to cardiovascular issues and inflammation.

- Pro-Inflammatory Properties: These fats can trigger inflammatory pathways within the body.

Alternatives:

- Choose healthier fats like olive oil, avocados, and nuts.

- Opt for lean protein sources, such as legumes and tofu.

- Limit the consumption of fried and heavily processed foods.

4. Excessive Dairy

While dairy can be a good source of nutrients, excessive consumption, especially of high-fat dairy products, may contribute to inflammation in some individuals.

Why Limit Excessive Dairy:

- Lactose Sensitivity: Some people may be lactose intolerant, experiencing digestive discomfort and inflammation after consuming dairy.

- Saturated Fat Content: Full-fat dairy products can be high in saturated fats, which may contribute to inflammation.

Alternatives:

- Choose low-fat or plant-based milk alternatives like almond, soy, or oat milk.

- Opt for plain, unsweetened yogurt and cheeses in moderation.

- Explore dairy-free alternatives for a lower-inflammatory impact.

Key Takeaway:

In a Vegetarian Anti-Inflammatory Diet, limiting or avoiding processed foods, refined sugar, saturated and trans fats, and excessive dairy can contribute to a reduction in inflammation. Instead, focus on incorporating whole, nutrient-dense foods, emphasizing fruits, vegetables, and plant-based protein sources for optimal health and well-being.

SECTION 1: BREAKFAST

1. Turmeric Spiced Oatmeal

Ingredients:

- 1 cup rolled oats

- 2 cups almond milk

- 1 teaspoon turmeric powder

- 1/2 teaspoon cinnamon

- 1 tablespoon maple syrup

- 1/4 cup chopped nuts (almonds, walnuts)

- Fresh fruit for topping (e.g., berries, banana slices)

Instructions:

1. In a saucepan, combine oats, almond milk, turmeric, and cinnamon.

2. Cook over medium heat, stirring occasionally until the oats are cooked and the mixture thickens.

3. Stir in maple syrup and top with nuts and fresh fruit.

Caloric Count (per serving): Approximately 300 calories

2. Avocado Toast with Cherry Tomatoes

Ingredients:

- 2 slices whole grain bread

- 1 ripe avocado

- Cherry tomatoes, sliced

- Red pepper flakes (optional)

- Salt and pepper to taste

Instructions:

1. Toast the bread slices.

2. Mash the ripe avocado and spread it evenly on the toasted bread.

3. Top with sliced cherry tomatoes, red pepper flakes (if desired), and season with salt and pepper.

Caloric Count (per serving): Approximately 250 calories

3. Chia Seed Pudding with Mixed Berries

Ingredients:

- 1/4 cup chia seeds

- 1 cup almond milk

- 1 tablespoon maple syrup

- 1/2 teaspoon vanilla extract

- Mixed berries for topping

Instructions:

1. In a jar, mix chia seeds, almond milk, maple syrup, and vanilla extract.

2. Stir well, cover, and refrigerate overnight.

3. Top with mixed berries before serving.

Caloric Count (per serving): Approximately 200 calories

4. Sweet Potato and Spinach Breakfast Burrito

Ingredients:

- 1 medium sweet potato, grated

- 1 cup fresh spinach

- 2 whole-grain tortillas

- 2 eggs, scrambled

- Salsa for topping

Instructions:

1. Saute grated sweet potato in a pan until softened.

2. Add fresh spinach and cook until wilted.

3. Scramble eggs and mix into the sweet potato and spinach mixture.

4. Divide the mixture between two tortillas, roll them up, and top with salsa.

Caloric Count (per serving) Approximately 350 calories

5. Quinoa Breakfast Bowl with Almond Milk

Ingredients:

- 1 cup cooked quinoa

- 1/2 cup sliced almonds

- Fresh fruit (e.g., berries, sliced banana)

- Almond milk for drizzling

- 1 tablespoon honey or maple syrup

Instructions:

1. In a bowl, layer cooked quinoa, sliced almonds, and fresh fruit.

2. Drizzle with almond milk and sweeten with honey or maple syrup.

Caloric Count (per serving): Approximately 320 calories

6. Lentil and Vegetable Soup

Ingredients:

- 1 cup dried lentils

- 4 cups vegetable broth

- 1 onion, diced

- 2 carrots, sliced

- 2 celery stalks, chopped

- 2 cloves garlic, minced

- 1 teaspoon cumin

- 1 teaspoon paprika

- Salt and pepper to taste

- Fresh parsley for garnish

Instructions:

1. Rinse lentils and combine them with vegetable broth in a pot.

2. Add diced onion, sliced carrots, chopped celery, minced garlic, cumin, paprika, salt, and pepper.

3. Bring to a boil, then reduce heat and simmer until lentils and vegetables are tender.

4. Garnish with fresh parsley before serving.

Caloric Count (per serving): Approximately 300 calories

7. Ginger Carrot Soup

Ingredients:

- 1 pound carrots, peeled and sliced

- 1 onion, chopped

- 2 tablespoons fresh ginger, grated

- 4 cups vegetable broth

- 1 cup coconut milk

- Salt and pepper to taste

- Fresh cilantro for garnish

Instructions:

1. In a pot, combine carrots, onion, ginger, and vegetable broth.

2. Bring to a boil, then reduce heat and simmer until carrots are tender.

3. Blend the soup until smooth, stir in coconut milk, and season with salt and pepper.

4. Garnish with fresh cilantro before serving.

Caloric Count (per serving): Approximately 220 calories

8. Tomato and Basil Gazpacho

Ingredients:

- 6 tomatoes, diced

- 1 cucumber, peeled and chopped

- 1 red bell pepper, chopped

- 2 cloves garlic, minced

- 1/4 cup red onion, chopped

- 3 cups tomato juice

- 1/4 cup fresh basil, chopped

- 2 tablespoons red wine vinegar

- Salt and pepper to taste

- Olive oil for drizzling (optional)

Instructions:

1. In a blender, combine tomatoes, cucumber, red bell pepper, garlic, red onion, tomato juice, basil, and red wine vinegar.

2. Blend until smooth, season with salt and pepper.

3. Chill in the refrigerator before serving.

4. Drizzle with olive oil if desired.

Caloric Count (per serving): Approximately 180 calories

9. Spicy Pumpkin Stew

Ingredients:

- 2 cups pumpkin, diced

- 1 can (15 oz) black beans, drained and rinsed

- 1 can (15 oz) diced tomatoes

- 1 onion, diced

- 2 cloves garlic, minced

- 1 tablespoon chili powder

- 1 teaspoon cumin

- Salt and pepper to taste

- Fresh cilantro for garnish

Instructions:

1. In a pot, combine pumpkin, black beans, diced tomatoes, onion, garlic, chili powder, cumin, salt, and pepper.

2. Bring to a simmer and cook until pumpkin is tender.

3. Garnish with fresh cilantro before serving.

Caloric Count (per serving): Approximately 250 calories

10. Spinach and White Bean Soup

Ingredients:

- 1 tablespoon olive oil

- 1 onion, chopped

- 2 carrots, sliced

- 2 celery stalks, chopped

- 2 cloves garlic, minced

- 4 cups vegetable broth

- 1 can (15 oz) white beans, drained and rinsed

- 2 cups fresh spinach

- 1 teaspoon dried thyme

- Salt and pepper to taste

- Lemon wedges for serving

Instructions:

1. In a pot, heat olive oil and sauté onion, carrots, celery, and garlic until softened.

2. Add vegetable broth, white beans, fresh spinach, thyme, salt, and pepper.

3. Simmer until the vegetables are tender.

4. Serve with lemon wedges.

Caloric Count (per serving): Approximately 280 calories

11. Kale and Quinoa Salad with Lemon-Tahini Dressing

Ingredients:

- 2 cups kale, chopped

- 1 cup cooked quinoa

- 1/2 cup cherry tomatoes, halved

- 1/4 cup cucumber, diced

- 1/4 cup red bell pepper, chopped

- 2 tablespoons pumpkin seeds

- 2 tablespoons feta cheese (optional)

Lemon-Tahini Dressing:

- 3 tablespoons tahini

- 2 tablespoons lemon juice

- 1 tablespoon olive oil

- 1 clove garlic, minced

- Salt and pepper to taste

Instructions:

1. In a large bowl, combine kale, cooked quinoa, cherry tomatoes, cucumber, red bell pepper, pumpkin seeds, and feta cheese.

2. In a small bowl, whisk together tahini, lemon juice, olive oil, garlic, salt, and pepper.

3. Pour the dressing over the salad and toss to combine.

Caloric Count (per serving): Approximately 320 calories

12. Broccoli and Walnut Salad

Ingredients:

- 2 cups broccoli florets, blanched

- 1/4 cup red onion, thinly sliced

- 1/4 cup dried cranberries

- 1/4 cup walnuts, chopped

- 1/4 cup feta cheese, crumbled

Lemon-Mustard Dressing:

- 2 tablespoons olive oil

- 1 tablespoon lemon juice

- 1 teaspoon Dijon mustard

- 1 teaspoon honey

- Salt and pepper to taste

Instructions:

1. In a bowl, combine blanched broccoli, red onion, dried cranberries, walnuts, and feta cheese.

2. In a small bowl, whisk together olive oil, lemon juice, Dijon mustard, honey, salt, and pepper.

3. Pour the dressing over the salad and toss to combine.

Caloric Count (per serving): Approximately 280 calories

13. Mediterranean Chickpea Salad

Ingredients:

- 1 can (15 oz) chickpeas, drained and rinsed

- 1 cucumber, diced

- 1 cup cherry tomatoes, halved

- 1/2 cup Kalamata olives, sliced

- 1/4 cup red onion, finely chopped

- 1/4 cup feta cheese, crumbled

Greek Dressing:

- 3 tablespoons olive oil

- 2 tablespoons red wine vinegar

- 1 teaspoon dried oregano

- Salt and pepper to taste

Instructions:

1. In a bowl, combine chickpeas, cucumber, cherry tomatoes, Kalamata olives, red onion, and feta cheese.

2. In a small bowl, whisk together olive oil, red wine vinegar, dried oregano, salt, and pepper.

3. Pour the dressing over the salad and toss to combine.

Caloric Count (per serving): Approximately 290 calories

14. Beet and Arugula Salad with Balsamic Vinaigrette

Ingredients:

- 2 medium beets, roasted and sliced

- 4 cups arugula

- 1/4 cup goat cheese, crumbled

- 1/4 cup walnuts, toasted

Balsamic Vinaigrette:

- 3 tablespoons balsamic vinegar

- 2 tablespoons olive oil

- 1 teaspoon Dijon mustard

- 1 teaspoon honey

- Salt and pepper to taste

Instructions:

1. Arrange roasted and sliced beets over a bed of arugula.

2. Sprinkle with goat cheese and toasted walnuts.

3. In a small bowl, whisk together balsamic vinegar, olive oil, Dijon mustard, honey, salt, and pepper.

4. Drizzle the vinaigrette over the salad.

Caloric Count (per serving): Approximately 260 calories

15. Cucumber Avocado Salad with Lime Dressing

Ingredients:

- 2 cucumbers, sliced

- 2 avocados, diced

- 1/4 cup red onion, thinly sliced

- 1/4 cup fresh cilantro, chopped

Lime Dressing:

- 3 tablespoons lime juice

- 2 tablespoons olive oil

- 1 teaspoon honey

- Salt and pepper to taste

Instructions:

1. In a bowl, combine sliced cucumbers, diced avocados, red onion, and cilantro.

2. In a small bowl, whisk together lime juice, olive oil, honey, salt, and pepper.

3. Pour the dressing over the salad and toss gently to coat.

Caloric Count (per serving): Approximately 230 calories

16. Roasted Vegetable Stir-Fry with Tofu

Ingredients:

- 1 block of firm tofu, pressed and cubed

- 2 cups broccoli florets

- 1 red bell pepper, sliced

- 1 yellow bell pepper, sliced

- 1 carrot, julienned

- 1 zucchini, sliced

- 2 tablespoons soy sauce

- 1 tablespoon sesame oil

- 1 tablespoon olive oil

- 1 teaspoon ginger, minced

- 2 cloves garlic, minced

- Salt and pepper to taste

Instructions:

1. Preheat the oven to 400°F (200°C).

2. Toss tofu with sesame oil and bake for 20-25 minutes or until golden.

3. In a large pan, heat olive oil over medium-high heat.

4. Add ginger and garlic, sauté for 1 minute.

5. Add broccoli, bell peppers, carrot, and zucchini. Stir-fry for 5-7 minutes.

6. Add baked tofu, soy sauce, salt, and pepper. Cook for an additional 2-3 minutes.

7. Serve over brown rice or quinoa.

Caloric Count: Approximately 300 calories per serving.

17. Cauliflower and Chickpea Curry

Ingredients:

- 1 cauliflower, cut into florets

- 1 can chickpeas, drained and rinsed

- 1 onion, diced

- 2 cloves garlic, minced

- 1 tablespoon curry powder

- 1 teaspoon turmeric

- 1 teaspoon cumin

- 1 can (14 oz) diced tomatoes

- 1 can (14 oz) coconut milk

- Salt and pepper to taste

- Fresh cilantro for garnish

Instructions:

1. In a large pot, sauté onion and garlic until translucent.

2. Add cauliflower, chickpeas, curry powder, turmeric, and cumin. Stir to coat.

3. Pour in diced tomatoes and coconut milk. Bring to a simmer.

4. Cover and cook for 20-25 minutes until cauliflower is tender.

5. Season with salt and pepper. Garnish with cilantro.

6. Serve over basmati rice or quinoa.

Caloric Count: Approximately 350 calories per serving.

18. Zucchini Noodles with Pesto

Ingredients:

- 4 medium-sized zucchinis, spiralized

- 1 cup cherry tomatoes, halved

- 1/2 cup pine nuts

- 2 cups fresh basil leaves

- 1/2 cup grated Parmesan cheese

- 2 cloves garlic

- 1/2 cup extra-virgin olive oil

- Salt and pepper to taste

Instructions:

1. In a blender or food processor, combine basil, pine nuts, garlic, and Parmesan.

2. Slowly add olive oil until smooth. Season with salt and pepper.

3. In a large pan, sauté zucchini noodles until just tender.

4. Toss zucchini noodles with pesto and cherry tomatoes.

5. Serve immediately.

Caloric Count: Approximately 250 calories per serving.

19. Sweet Potato and Black Bean Enchiladas

Ingredients:

- 2 large sweet potatoes, peeled and diced

- 1 can black beans, drained and rinsed

- 1 red onion, diced

- 1 red bell pepper, diced

- 8 whole wheat tortillas

- 1 cup enchilada sauce

- 1 cup shredded vegan cheese

- Fresh cilantro for garnish

Instructions:

1. Preheat the oven to 375°F (190°C).

2. Steam sweet potatoes until tender. Mash them in a bowl.

3. Add black beans, red onion, and bell pepper to the mashed sweet potatoes.

4. Spoon the mixture onto tortillas and roll them up.

5. Place rolled tortillas in a baking dish and cover with enchilada sauce and vegan cheese.

6. Bake for 20-25 minutes until cheese is melted and bubbly.

7. Garnish with fresh cilantro and serve.

Caloric Count: Approximately 400 calories per serving.

20. Eggplant and Mushroom Lasagna

Ingredients:

- 1 large eggplant, thinly sliced

- 2 cups mushrooms, sliced

- 2 cups spinach

- 1 jar marinara sauce

- 9 whole wheat lasagna noodles, cooked

- 2 cups ricotta cheese (or tofu for a vegan option)

- 1 cup shredded mozzarella cheese (or vegan cheese)

- Fresh basil for garnish

Instructions:

1. Preheat the oven to 375°F (190°C).

2. In a pan, sauté mushrooms until browned. Add spinach and cook until wilted.

3. In a baking dish, layer marinara sauce, lasagna noodles, eggplant, ricotta, mushroom-spinach mixture, and mozzarella.

4. Repeat layers, finishing with a layer of marinara and mozzarella.

5. Cover with foil and bake for 30 minutes. Remove foil and bake for an additional 15 minutes until bubbly.

6. Garnish with fresh basil and let it cool before serving.

Caloric Count: Approximately 450 calories per serving.

SECTION 5: SIDES

21. Garlic Roasted Brussels Sprouts

Ingredients:

- 1 lb Brussels sprouts, trimmed and halved

- 3 tablespoons olive oil

- 4 cloves garlic, minced

- Salt and pepper to taste

Instructions:

1. Preheat the oven to 400°F (200°C).

2. Toss Brussels sprouts with olive oil, garlic, salt, and pepper.

3. Spread them on a baking sheet in a single layer.

4. Roast for 20-25 minutes or until crispy and browned.

5. Serve hot.

Caloric Count: Approximately 100 calories per serving.

22. Turmeric Roasted Cauliflower

Ingredients:

- 1 head cauliflower, cut into florets

- 2 tablespoons olive oil

- 1 teaspoon turmeric

- 1 teaspoon cumin

- Salt and pepper to taste

Instructions:

1. Preheat the oven to 425°F (220°C).

2. Toss cauliflower with olive oil, turmeric, cumin, salt, and pepper.

3. Spread on a baking sheet and roast for 25-30 minutes until golden.

4. Serve as a side dish.

Caloric Count: Approximately 120 calories per serving.

23. Quinoa and Vegetable Stuffed Peppers

Ingredients:

- 4 bell peppers, halved and seeds removed

- 1 cup quinoa, cooked

- 1 can black beans, drained and rinsed

- 1 cup corn kernels

- 1 cup cherry tomatoes, diced

- 1 teaspoon cumin

- 1 teaspoon chili powder

- Salt and pepper to taste

- 1 cup shredded cheddar cheese (optional)

Instructions:

1. Preheat the oven to 375°F (190°C).

2. In a bowl, mix quinoa, black beans, corn, tomatoes, cumin, chili powder, salt, and pepper.

3. Stuff the pepper halves with the quinoa mixture.

4. Place stuffed peppers in a baking dish, cover with foil, and bake for 25-30 minutes.

5. If using cheese, sprinkle it over the peppers in the last 5 minutes of baking.

6. Serve hot.

Caloric Count: Approximately 250 calories per serving.

24. Lemon Herb Roasted Potatoes

Ingredients:

- 2 lbs baby potatoes, halved

- 3 tablespoons olive oil

- Zest and juice of 1 lemon

- 1 teaspoon dried thyme

- 1 teaspoon dried rosemary

- Salt and pepper to taste

Instructions:

1. Preheat the oven to 400°F (200°C).

2. Toss potatoes with olive oil, lemon zest, lemon juice, thyme, rosemary, salt, and pepper.

3. Spread on a baking sheet and roast for 30-35 minutes or until golden.

4. Serve as a flavorful side dish.

Caloric Count: Approximately 150 calories per serving.

25. Sauteed Green Beans with Almonds

Ingredients:

- 1 lb green beans, trimmed

- 2 tablespoons olive oil

- 1/4 cup sliced almonds

- 2 cloves garlic, minced

- Salt and pepper to taste

- Lemon wedges for garnish

Instructions:

1. Blanch green beans in boiling water for 2-3 minutes. Drain and set aside.

2. In a pan, heat olive oil over medium heat.

3. Add sliced almonds and sauté until golden.

4. Add minced garlic and sauté for 1 minute.

5. Add green beans, toss until coated and heated through.

6. Season with salt and pepper.

7. Garnish with lemon wedges and serve.

Caloric Count: Approximately 120 calories per serving.

26. Hummus and Veggie Sticks

Ingredients:

- 1 can chickpeas, drained and rinsed

- 1/4 cup tahini

- 1/4 cup olive oil

- 1 clove garlic, minced

- Juice of 1 lemon

- Salt and pepper to taste

- Carrot and cucumber sticks for dipping

Instructions:

1. In a food processor, blend chickpeas, tahini, olive oil, garlic, lemon juice, salt, and pepper until smooth.

2. Adjust seasoning if necessary.

3. Serve with fresh carrot and cucumber sticks.

Caloric Count: Approximately 100 calories per serving.

27. Spiced Nuts Mix

Ingredients:

- 1 cup mixed nuts (almonds, walnuts, cashews)

- 1 tablespoon olive oil

- 1 teaspoon cumin

- 1 teaspoon paprika

- 1/2 teaspoon cayenne pepper

- Salt to taste

Instructions:

1. Preheat the oven to 350°F (180°C).

2. Toss nuts with olive oil, cumin, paprika, cayenne pepper, and salt.

3. Spread on a baking sheet and roast for 10-15 minutes, stirring occasionally.

4. Let them cool before serving.

Caloric Count: Approximately 150 calories per serving.

28. Roasted Chickpeas with Herbs

Ingredients:

- 2 cans chickpeas, drained and rinsed

- 2 tablespoons olive oil

- 1 teaspoon cumin

- 1 teaspoon smoked paprika

- 1/2 teaspoon garlic powder

- Salt and pepper to taste

Instructions:

1. Preheat the oven to 400°F (200°C).

2. Toss chickpeas with olive oil, cumin, paprika, garlic powder, salt, and pepper.

3. Spread on a baking sheet and roast for 25-30 minutes until crispy.

4. Allow them to cool before serving.

Caloric Count: Approximately 120 calories per serving.

29. Guacamole with Whole Grain Crackers

Ingredients:

- 3 ripe avocados, mashed

- 1 tomato, diced

- 1/4 cup red onion, finely chopped

- 1 clove garlic, minced

- Juice of 1 lime

- Salt and pepper to taste

- Whole grain crackers for serving

Instructions:

1. In a bowl, combine mashed avocados, tomato, red onion, garlic, lime juice, salt, and pepper.

2. Mix well and adjust seasoning if necessary.

3. Serve with whole grain crackers.

Caloric Count: Approximately 150 calories per serving.

30. Greek Yogurt and Berry Parfait

Ingredients:

- 1 cup Greek yogurt

- 1 cup mixed berries (strawberries, blueberries, raspberries)

- 1/4 cup granola

- 1 tablespoon honey

Instructions:

1. In a glass or bowl, layer Greek yogurt, mixed berries, and granola.

2. Drizzle honey on top.

3. Repeat layers if desired.

4. Serve chilled.

Caloric Count: Approximately 200 calories per serving.

31. Turmeric Golden Milk Latte

Ingredients:

- 1 cup almond milk

- 1 tsp turmeric powder

- 1/2 tsp cinnamon

- 1/4 tsp ginger powder

- 1 tsp honey or maple syrup (optional)

Instructions:

1. In a small saucepan, heat almond milk over medium heat.

2. Whisk in turmeric, cinnamon, and ginger until well combined.

3. Heat until warm but not boiling.

4. Sweeten with honey or maple syrup if desired.

Caloric Count (per serving): Approximately 80 calories

32. Green Tea and Ginger Cooler

Ingredients:

- 2 green tea bags

- 1-inch fresh ginger, sliced

- 1 tbsp honey

- Ice cubes

Instructions:

1. Steep green tea bags in hot water for 3-5 minutes.

2. Add ginger slices to the tea and let it cool.

3. Stir in honey until dissolved.

4. Refrigerate and serve over ice.

Caloric Count (per serving): Approximately 10 calories

33. Cucumber Mint Infused Water

Ingredients:

- 1/2 cucumber, thinly sliced

- 1/4 cup fresh mint leaves

- Ice cubes

- Water

Instructions:

1. Combine cucumber slices and mint leaves in a pitcher.

2. Add ice cubes and fill the pitcher with water.

3. Refrigerate for at least 2 hours before serving.

Caloric Count (per serving): Negligible (virtually zero calories)

34. Berry Smoothie with Flaxseeds

Ingredients:

- 1 cup mixed berries (strawberries, blueberries, raspberries)

- 1 banana

- 1 cup almond milk

- 1 tbsp flaxseeds

- Ice cubes

Instructions:

1. Blend berries, banana, almond milk, and flaxseeds until smooth.

2. Add ice cubes and blend again until desired consistency.

Caloric Count (per serving): Approximately 150 calories

35. Anti-Inflammatory Green Juice

Ingredients:

- 2 cups kale

- 1 cucumber

- 1 green apple

- 1-inch ginger

- 1 lemon, peeled

Instructions:

1. Run all ingredients through a juicer.

2. Stir well and serve over ice if desired.

Caloric Count (per serving): Approximately 80 calories

36. Turmeric Coconut Bliss Balls

Ingredients:

- 1 cup dates, pitted

- 1/2 cup almonds

- 1/4 cup shredded coconut

- 1 tsp turmeric powder

- 1/2 tsp vanilla extract

Instructions:

1. Blend dates, almonds, coconut, turmeric, and vanilla in a food processor until a sticky dough forms.

2. Roll the mixture into bite-sized balls.

3. Optional: Roll in additional coconut or turmeric for coating.

Caloric Count (per serving): Approximately 80 calories per ball (makes about 12 balls)

37. Dark Chocolate Avocado Mousse

Ingredients:

- 2 ripe avocados

- 1/4 cup cocoa powder

- 1/4 cup maple syrup

- 1 tsp vanilla extract

- A pinch of salt

Instructions:

1. Blend avocados, cocoa powder, maple syrup, vanilla, and salt until smooth.

2. Refrigerate for at least 2 hours before serving.

Caloric Count (per serving): Approximately 150 calories

38. Blueberry Chia Seed Pudding

Ingredients:

- 1/2 cup blueberries

- 2 tbsp chia seeds

- 1 cup almond milk

- 1 tbsp maple syrup

- 1/2 tsp vanilla extract

Instructions:

1. Mash blueberries and mix with chia seeds, almond milk, maple syrup, and vanilla.

2. Refrigerate overnight or until the pudding thickens.

Caloric Count (per serving): Approximately 120 calories

39. Mango Sorbet with Mint

Ingredients:

- 2 cups frozen mango chunks

- 1/4 cup fresh mint leaves

- 1 tbsp lime juice

- 2 tbsp agave syrup

Instructions:

1. Blend mango, mint, lime juice, and agave syrup until smooth.

2. Freeze for 2-3 hours before serving.

Caloric Count (per serving): Approximately 100 calories

40. Almond Flour Banana Bread

Ingredients:

- 2 ripe bananas, mashed

- 3 eggs

- 1/4 cup coconut oil

- 1/4 cup almond milk

- 1 tsp vanilla extract

- 2 cups almond flour

- 1/2 tsp baking soda

- 1/4 tsp salt

Instructions:

1. Preheat the oven to 350°F (175°C) and grease a loaf pan.

2. In a bowl, mix mashed bananas, eggs, coconut oil, almond milk, and vanilla.

3. Add almond flour, baking soda, and salt. Mix until well combined.

4. Pour the batter into the loaf pan and bake for 45-50 minutes.

Caloric Count (per serving): Approximately 200 calories (12 slices per loaf)

46. Spaghetti Squash with Roasted Tomatoes and Basil

Ingredients:

- 1 medium-sized spaghetti squash

- 2 cups cherry tomatoes, halved

- 1/4 cup fresh basil, chopped

- 2 cloves garlic, minced

- 2 tablespoons olive oil

- Salt and pepper to taste

- Parmesan cheese for garnish (optional)

Instructions:

1. Preheat the oven to 400°F (200°C).

2. Cut the spaghetti squash in half lengthwise, scoop out the seeds, and place them cut side down on a baking sheet.

3. In a bowl, toss the cherry tomatoes, garlic, basil, olive oil, salt, and pepper.

4. Spread the tomato mixture on a separate baking sheet.

5. Roast both the spaghetti squash and tomatoes in the oven for 30-40 minutes, or until squash is tender and tomatoes are caramelized.

6. Scrape the spaghetti squash strands into a bowl, top with roasted tomatoes, and garnish with Parmesan cheese if desired.

Caloric Count (per serving): Approximately 150 calories

47. Lemon Garlic Orzo with Asparagus

Ingredients:

- 1 cup orzo pasta

- 1 bunch asparagus, trimmed and cut into bite-sized pieces

- 2 cloves garlic, minced

- Zest and juice of 1 lemon

- 2 tablespoons olive oil

- Salt and pepper to taste

- Fresh parsley for garnish

Instructions:

1. Cook orzo according to package instructions. Drain and set aside.

2. In a large skillet, heat olive oil over medium heat. Add garlic and sauté until fragrant.

3. Add asparagus to the skillet and cook until tender-crisp.

4. Stir in cooked orzo, lemon zest, and lemon juice. Season with salt and pepper.

5. Garnish with fresh parsley before serving.

Caloric Count (per serving): Approximately 250 calories

48. Mushroom and Spinach Risotto

Ingredients:

- 1 cup Arborio rice

- 1/2 cup dry white wine

- 4 cups vegetable broth, kept warm

- 1 cup mushrooms, sliced

- 2 cups baby spinach

- 1 onion, finely chopped

- 2 cloves garlic, minced

- 2 tablespoons olive oil

- 1/2 cup Parmesan cheese, grated

- Salt and pepper to taste

Instructions:

1. In a large pan, sauté onions and garlic in olive oil until softened.

2. Add Arborio rice and cook for 2-3 minutes until lightly toasted.

3. Pour in the white wine and cook until it evaporates.

4. Gradually add warm vegetable broth, one ladle at a time, stirring frequently until absorbed.

5. Continue adding broth and stirring until the rice is creamy and cooked al dente.

6. Stir in mushrooms and spinach until wilted.

7. Remove from heat, stir in Parmesan cheese, and season with salt and pepper.

Caloric Count (per serving): Approximately 350 calories

49. Pesto Zucchini Noodles with Cherry Tomatoes

Ingredients:

- 4 medium zucchini, spiralized

- 1 cup cherry tomatoes, halved

- 1/3 cup basil pesto

- 2 tablespoons pine nuts

- Salt and pepper to taste

- Grated Parmesan cheese for garnish (optional)

Instructions:

1. Spiralize the zucchini into noodles.

2. In a large skillet, sauté zucchini noodles until just tender.

3. Add cherry tomatoes and cook for an additional 2-3 minutes.

4. Stir in basil pesto and pine nuts, tossing to coat.

5. Season with salt and pepper.

6. Garnish with Parmesan cheese if desired.

Caloric Count (per serving): Approximately 180 calories

50. Quinoa and Black Bean Stuffed Bell Peppers

Ingredients:

- 4 large bell peppers, halved and seeds removed

- 1 cup quinoa, cooked

- 1 can black beans, drained and rinsed

- 1 cup corn kernels (fresh or frozen)

- 1 cup diced tomatoes

- 1 teaspoon cumin

- 1 teaspoon chili powder

- Salt and pepper to taste

- 1 cup shredded Mexican cheese blend

- Fresh cilantro for garnish

Instructions:

1. Preheat the oven to 375°F (190°C).

2. In a bowl, mix together cooked quinoa, black beans, corn, tomatoes, cumin, chili powder, salt, and pepper.

3. Stuff each bell pepper half with the quinoa mixture.

4. Place the stuffed peppers in a baking dish and sprinkle with shredded cheese.

5. Bake for 25-30 minutes or until the peppers are tender and the cheese is melted.

6. Garnish with fresh cilantro before serving.

Caloric Count (per serving): Approximately 300 calories

51. Grilled Portobello Mushroom Wrap

Ingredients:

- 4 large portobello mushrooms, cleaned and sliced

- 1 red bell pepper, sliced

- 1 red onion, sliced

- 2 tablespoons balsamic vinegar

- 2 tablespoons olive oil

- Salt and pepper to taste

- Whole grain wraps

- Hummus for spreading

Instructions:

1. Preheat the grill or grill pan over medium-high heat.

2. In a bowl, toss the portobello mushrooms, bell pepper, and red onion with balsamic vinegar, olive oil, salt, and pepper.

3. Grill the vegetables until tender and slightly charred.

4. Spread hummus on whole grain wraps, and fill with grilled vegetables.

5. Roll the wraps and secure with toothpicks if needed.

Caloric Count (per serving): Approximately 200 calories

52. Chickpea Salad Sandwich with Avocado

Ingredients:

- 1 can chickpeas, drained and rinsed

- 1/4 cup vegan mayonnaise

- 1 celery stalk, finely chopped

- 1/4 red onion, finely chopped

- 1 tablespoon Dijon mustard

- Salt and pepper to taste

- Whole grain bread

- Avocado slices and lettuce for sandwich filling

Instructions:

1. In a bowl, mash chickpeas with a fork.

2. Add vegan mayonnaise, celery, red onion, Dijon mustard, salt, and pepper. Mix well.

3. Toast whole grain bread slices.

4. Spread chickpea salad on one slice, top with avocado slices and lettuce, and cover with another slice of bread.

Caloric Count (per serving): Approximately 250 calories

53. Mediterranean Veggie Wrap

Ingredients:

- Whole grain wraps

- 1 cup hummus

- 1 cucumber, thinly sliced

- 1 tomato, sliced

- 1/2 red onion, thinly sliced

- Kalamata olives, pitted and sliced

- Feta cheese, crumbled

- Fresh parsley, chopped

Instructions:

1. Spread a generous layer of hummus on each whole grain wrap.

2. Layer cucumber, tomato, red onion, olives, feta cheese, and parsley on top.

3. Roll up the wraps and secure with toothpicks if needed.

Caloric Count (per serving): Approximately 300 calories

54. Caprese Sandwich with Balsamic Glaze

Ingredients:

- Whole grain bread

- 1 large tomato, sliced

- Fresh mozzarella, sliced

- Fresh basil leaves

- Balsamic glaze

- Salt and pepper to taste

Instructions:

1. Toast whole grain bread slices.

2. Layer tomato slices, mozzarella slices, and fresh basil leaves on the bread.

3. Drizzle with balsamic glaze and season with salt and pepper.

Caloric Count (per serving): Approximately 250 calories

55. Avocado and Hummus Veggie Wrap

Ingredients:

- Whole grain wraps

- Hummus for spreading

- 1 avocado, sliced

- 1 bell pepper, thinly sliced

- 1 carrot, julienned

- Spinach leaves

Instructions:

1. Spread a layer of hummus on each whole grain wrap.

2. Arrange avocado slices, bell pepper, carrot, and spinach leaves on the wraps.

3. Roll up the wraps and secure with toothpicks if needed.

Caloric Count (per serving): Approximately 280 calories

56. Cauliflower Crust Pizza with Roasted Vegetables

Ingredients:

- 1 cauliflower head, grated

- 2 eggs

- 1 teaspoon dried oregano

- 1 teaspoon garlic powder

- Salt and pepper to taste

- Pizza sauce

- Mozzarella cheese

- Assorted roasted vegetables (e.g., bell peppers, cherry tomatoes, zucchini)

Instructions:

1. Preheat the oven to 400°F (200°C).

2. Mix grated cauliflower, eggs, oregano, garlic powder, salt, and pepper in a bowl.

3. Press the mixture into a pizza crust shape on a baking sheet lined with parchment paper.

4. Bake for 20-25 minutes or until the crust is golden.

5. Spread pizza sauce on the crust, add mozzarella cheese, and top with roasted vegetables.

6. Bake for an additional 10-15 minutes or until the cheese is melted and bubbly.

Caloric Count (per serving): Approximately 220 calories

57. Mediterranean Pizza with Olives and Feta

Ingredients:

- Whole wheat pizza dough

- Olive oil

- Pizza sauce

- Mozzarella cheese

- Kalamata olives, pitted and sliced

- Feta cheese, crumbled

- Fresh oregano

Instructions:

1. Preheat the oven according to the pizza dough package instructions.

2. Roll out the pizza dough on a floured surface and transfer to a pizza stone or baking sheet.

3. Brush the crust with olive oil.

4. Spread pizza sauce, mozzarella cheese, olives, and feta cheese on the dough.

5. Bake according to the pizza dough package instructions.

6. Garnish with fresh oregano before serving.

Caloric Count (per serving): Approximately 280 calories

58. Spinach and Artichoke Pizza

Ingredients:

- Whole wheat pizza dough

- Olive oil

- Pizza sauce

- Mozzarella cheese

- Fresh spinach, chopped

- Artichoke hearts, chopped

- Garlic, minced

Instructions:

1. Preheat the oven according to the pizza dough package instructions.

2. Roll out the pizza dough on a floured surface and transfer to a pizza stone or baking sheet.

3. Brush the crust with olive oil.

4. Spread pizza sauce, mozzarella cheese, chopped spinach, artichoke hearts, and minced garlic on the dough.

5. Bake according to the pizza dough package instructions.

Caloric Count (per serving): Approximately 250 calories

59. Margherita Pizza with Whole Wheat Crust

Ingredients:

- Whole wheat pizza dough

- Olive oil

- Pizza sauce

- Fresh mozzarella, sliced

- Fresh tomatoes, sliced

- Fresh basil leaves

Instructions:

1. Preheat the oven according to the pizza dough package instructions.

2. Roll out the pizza dough on a floured surface and transfer to a pizza stone or baking sheet.

3. Brush the crust with olive oil.

4. Spread pizza sauce, fresh mozzarella slices, and tomato slices on the dough.

5. Bake according to the pizza dough package instructions.

6. Garnish with fresh basil leaves before serving.

Caloric Count (per serving): Approximately 260 calories

60. Sweet Potato and Kale Pizza

Ingredients:

- Whole wheat pizza dough

- Olive oil

- Pizza sauce

- Mozzarella cheese

- Sweet potato, thinly sliced

- Kale, stems removed and chopped

- Red onion, thinly sliced

**Instruction

1. Preheat the oven according to the pizza dough package instructions.

2. Roll out the pizza dough on a floured surface and transfer to a pizza stone or baking sheet.

3. Brush the crust with olive oil.

4. Spread pizza sauce, mozzarella cheese, sweet potato slices, chopped kale, and red onion on the dough.

5. Bake according to the pizza dough package instructions.

Caloric Count (per serving): Approximately 270 calories